Climb to the Peak

How to write your vision

and develop a plan

to achieve your greatest dreams

Dr Todd William Dearing

Copyright © 2024 Todd William Dearing. All rights reserved.

First published 2024 by
Genius Authoring Pty Ltd (ACN 669 120 978)
Canberra, Australian Capital Territory

www.geniusauthoring.com.au

No part of this publication may be reproduced, stored in a retrieval system, or transmitted in any form or by any means, electronic, mechanical, photocopying, recording, or otherwise, without the prior written permission of the publisher and copyright holder.

ISBN: 978-1-7635145-0-8

Written, designed, and edited by Dr Todd William Dearing.

 A catalogue record for this book is available from the National Library of Australia

Any enquiries regarding this publication can be directed to enquiries@geniusauthoring.com.au.

Disclaimer

While this product is intended to help you clarify and achieve your goals in life and develop your greater human potential, this book and any information contained herein is general in nature. The provision of this product does not take into account your personal circumstances or specific goals.

All information provided by Genius Authoring and the author is not intended to be financial or medical advice of any kind and should not be relied upon as such. Many factors will be important in determining whether you achieve the goals you have set when acquiring and using this product, and there is no guarantee that you will be able to reach any of these aforementioned goals within any timeframe or at all.

You should obtain appropriate financial, legal and other professional advice before relying on the information provided by us. We make no representation or guarantee that this product will be useful or relevant to you or that applying any ideas, recommendations, methods or techniques we provide to you will achieve any particular outcomes.

For full terms and conditions applicable to our products and services, please visit www.geniusauthoring.com.au/terms-and-conditions

There is a genius
in every man and woman,
waiting to be brought forth.

– Wallace D Wattles

Contents

SECTION 1—CLIMB TO THE PEAK   **6**

    Introduction   8
    How to use this book   11
    Aim for the stars   13
    The author's story   14

SECTION 2—WRITE YOUR VISION   **22**

    What is your big dream?   24
    Create, explore, clarify   27
    The powerhouse of why   30
    Unpacking your ultimate dream   33

SECTION 3—FORM YOUR GOALS   **36**

    Concrete, achievable steps   38
    The obstacles make it real   41
    Knowing what is reliable   44
    Steps and milestones   46
    Navigating through analysis   50

SECTION 4—PREPARE FOR ACTION 70

    The art of turning dreams into reality 72

    Recalibrate at the milestones 84

    You're going to want to quit 86

    Imagine your wiser self into action 88

    Transform into your greater potential 91

    Building imagination into the concrete 92

    It's time to reshape the nest, or leave 94

    Self-imposed limits 96

    The time to climb is now 98

EXTRAS 102

    Epilogue: The peak is forever 104

    Reader reflections 106

    References 115

    Author bio 116

    Genius Authoring 117

Section 1
Climb to the peak

Introduction

To dream of the great things you'd like to do in life is natural. Whether or not we take these dreams seriously, and whether we follow through with action, against all obstacles, is another matter.

No doubt you've had your small dreams—the wish to be accepted into a specific course at university, wanting to date a certain guy or girl, yearning to explore a distant country, perhaps something else. Maybe you reached these dreams—if you did, you will know the feeling of turning a vision into a reality. While the reality is often not exactly what you imagined, there's a satisfaction from achieving what you set out to do.

Research into psychology shows that humans feel satisfaction when pursuing a goal and making progress on it.[1] This satisfaction is the reward that further motivates us toward that goal. We feel a sense of meaning, purpose, and well-being as we pursue a goal—even before reaching it. Moreover, the bigger the goal, the more satisfaction and excitement we feel as we progress toward it.

You are likely to have had some big dreams. At some point, you may have even chased after them. Yet perhaps they didn't work out. Those around you, even those closest to you, might have discouraged you from pursuing your dreams: "It's not possible. You're too ambitious. Temper your enthusiasm. Be realistic. Don't waste your time."

Like breaker waves pushing the determined swimmer back to the shore, on and on attempts come to keep you average, always from those who've never pursued their own big dreams, or have attempted such but had their hopes squashed. They have settled for an ordinary life and want you to do the same. Such people will do anything to keep you like them, because your success would only highlight the disappointment and feelings of inadequacy that they took on in exchange for abandoning their dreams.

But their words of discouragement grate against you. Why? Because you know there is something more real inside you, something greater to be achieved. You know you can do it, given the chance.

This book is a chance, an invitation to truly go for what is most important to you in life. Your big dreams call to you as your true destiny.

We live in an age where words like 'destiny' are shunned. To accept its meaning requires an individual to acknowledge, for a start, that life has meaning and purpose. Not long ago, and for many millennia prior, such ideas were entirely normal. Now they've been intellectually deconstructed, rationalised away.

I'm not suggesting that you subscribe to any particular worldview around the idea of destiny, but I am quite certain that most people want some form of purpose and meaning in their lives, even if entirely invented. Psychologists have shown that people with purpose and meaning in their lives have greater well-being and resilience,[2,3] while those lacking purpose and meaning tend to experience more depression, anxiety, and other psychological pathologies.[4] We are geared to achieve important things in life.

The term destiny is from the Latin *dēstināre*, 'to make firm; to establish' or 'to aim at' (as an archery term). It provides a sense of something's completion; to hit the mark, to firmly establish something as what it truly is. For a project, a business, a goal, this is to fulfil its proper completion. For a person, such as yourself, it is to manifest one's full potential—to become self-actualised. Each of us fulfils our destiny in our own unique and self-determined manner.

Now, let's assume that if you're reading this book, an average life is not your primary aim. Let's assume you have at least one big dream, as well as some smaller ones. You may not know what that big dream is yet—that's part of what this book is for.

This book is designed to aid you in making your dreams a reality. Yet it's not some miracle manifestation guide. It provides pragmatic guided writing activities that you can work on to clarify your vision, set your plans, and act toward your destiny. The dream, the effort, and the responsibility for the outcome are all yours. So is the incredible sense of purpose and deep satisfaction that come from pursuing and ultimately achieving your dreams.

In pursuing your greatest dreams you are climbing to the peak within yourself. You are writing your own destiny. This is not easy. If it were, you would already be there. It is challenging and it is transformative, and it requires qualities such as courage, discipline, responsibility, initiative, and perseverance.

Yet this journey's rewards are deeply enriching and enduring. In the process you will gain knowledge, develop your skills, and greatly expand your understanding of life and yourself. You will experience deeper meaning and purpose. You will bring value to others. And most importantly, you will become more of who you truly are.

If you haven't been repelled yet, then maybe you have what it takes to really go for it. Not sure? Don't worry—this book will help you become clearer about what you want and how to reach it.

In such beginnings are the seed of what will one day be a magnificent tree; your dreams made real by your own endeavour.

How to use this book

This book is a guide to assist you in achieving the big dreams in your life. Each section is a step in the process of defining, planning, and achieving a big dream.

Once you finish a section, I recommend taking a break before starting the next—be it an hour, a day, or longer. This is to allow time to reflect on what you've recently completed, as a transition into the next section. To support this transition, each section finishes with a reflection point.

This book is practical. It includes activities for you to complete: questions, writing exercises, and other instructions, all of which are instrumental in getting the most out of this book. Do the activities at your own pace.

> **Download your free PDF** containing all the activities in this book by joining the Genius Authoring mailing list at:
>
> www.geniusauthoring.com.au/cttp-activities
>
> You can fill out this PDF as you work through the activities, either in digital or printed form, as you prefer. You can also copy this PDF so that you can repeat the activities as many times as you need.
>
> Activities are numbered in this main book as a red circle:
>
> You will find the corresponding activity number in the PDF.

I also recommend having a separate notebook for any additional notes and ideas that arise as you work through the activities.

This book's process is iterative. It is designed to help you gradually clarify an understanding about how to achieve your goals. Don't expect perfect results immediately. You may need to complete some activities several times before things fall into place.

Be aware of the time you will need to complete this book. While you may finish all activities in a day, a week, or a month, the actual fulfilment of your end-goal—the achievement of your big dream through actionable steps—could take years, depending on what it is. This is perfectly fine, as most things worth doing take time. During this journey, you can return to what you wrote in these pages.

You can also redo the activities at any time. While your end goal might not change, once you've gained some experience working toward it, you might find it useful to refresh or update your vision, plans, and actions.

There are, however, two extremes in this process that should be avoided. The first is overthinking—analysis paralysis. Spend enough time thinking and planning toward your goal, but once that is done, if you do not act on those plans, nothing will come of it. Don't let theory be an excuse to avoid real action.

The other extreme is acting without a clear vision or plan. This can result in doing a lot but getting nowhere, which can leave one frustrated and exhausted, with resources depleted. Planning and action need to be a well-integrated pair, each relying on each other's strengths. With mind and body capable, coherent, and combined, you will stay on the balanced path that will ensure you have the greatest chance of success.

Aim for the stars

What exactly is a 'big dream'? Simply put, it's something big that you dream of achieving in your life.

Here's some examples: starting a company, helping a local community, buying a home, running a farm-to-table café, a career in film, becoming a sports superstar, becoming the mayor of your city, gaining ten million dollars, travelling to 100 different countries, raising a family, becoming fluent in a language, travelling into space, writing a book, mastering the violin, inventing a new technology, or anything else that is amazing, meaningful, inspiring, beneficial, worthwhile, big, purposeful, and so on.

These examples are to get you thinking, not to be copied. Be sure to go your own way and explore what is uniquely true for you. The big dream to pursue must be *your* big dream.

You may not know what your dream is yet. Perhaps you have a vague idea. Or perhaps you know what you are aiming at and are looking for a supportive framework to reach it. In any of these cases, this book will help you move toward your greater purpose.

Whatever you do, do not sell yourself short. Aim for the stars and you will make it at least to the moon.

STORIES OF REAL SUCCESS

As you work through this book, you should seek out the many stories of real people who have chosen above all else to pursue their own unique dreams and have succeeded. Look for those people who lure your interest. Read their bibliographies, listen to their advice, learn from their examples. They can inspire you too to recognise that there is a peak inside you waiting to be climbed.

The author's story

Looking around and seeing little practical guidance on writing a clear vision and developing a plan to achieve one's greatest dreams, I decided to write this book, and subtitle it as such. But how did I come to this—not the subtitle—and why? So that you can understand what's behind this book, I'd like to share my own story about big dreams.

THE GREAT ADVENTURE OF A DEEPLY CURIOUS INDIVIDUAL

Growing up in Adelaide, Australia, convinced me that my early life was more or less like ever other kid's. I liked to have fun, play sport, eat food, and watch all the regular TV shows—at least on the outside.

But there was always this other thread of deep curiosity that ran through my days. This stood out for me because it taught me to act from my own initiative. It led me to pursue with unequalled focus those things that deeply interested me, sourced from the environment around me. This included reading as many books as I could find in libraries—about science, computing, ancient mysteries, and fantasy novels, among other topics—and teaching myself to code in BASIC and machine language—to create games, understand 3D-modelling and colour palettes, and demonstrate physics models on our first home computer.

My curiosity also inspired an interest in role-playing games (the pen and paper kind originally) because these involved active imagination, storytelling, rich systems of character development, echoes of medieval history, technical fictional lore, and dice. I was almost always the Dungeon Master. While I often longed to play a character, I also enjoyed creating detailed worlds, scenarios, and quests for the other players to experience. Later, I focused on world building in multi-player online roleplaying games.

When I discovered my older sister's high school maths books (3 years above me), the thread of deep curiosity ensured I bring myself to understand those intriguing mathematical functions and processes, the various buttons on a scientific calculator, and how all this could be used in computer coding. A few years later, combining top grades in physics and maths with my parents' encouragement ("You're good at it," they said), I enrolled in a science degree—physics, mathematics, computer science—at university. I typically did the minimum work necessary, finished exams in half the time and left early, and still received very good grades. I loved understanding how the physical world worked. The connection between mathematics and the world came naturally to me. Physics demonstrated the precise relationships between sub-atomic particles and gigantic stars; mathematics presented both the orderly maps of vector-calculus and the beautiful, chaotic patterns of fractal geometry; and computers were the ultimate device for calculating and representing all this.

But equally as I expanded my grasp of the physical and mathematical worlds, deeper questions arose. I could see how science was useful in numerous ways, but it couldn't adequately explain consciousness. Science explained *how* the world worked, but not *who* I was. Thus I turned again to the library, this time at university, with access to a full range of academic books on every conceivable topic. I read widely on consciousness, mythology, psychology, spirituality, religion, folklore, shamanic traditions, Buddhism, yoga, and other topics. At the same time, I spent a great amount of time walking, wandering the national parks of the area and contemplating the natural world.

Then one morning, no doubt at the invitation of that curiosity within,

I woke up and decided to start meditating. I was 18 at the time. Since then, I have practised meditation every day of my life.

Eventually, I convinced myself that I didn't want to become an astrophysicist, as I had planned, spending all day looking through telescopes and staring at screens in an observatory. I began to explore various Buddhist traditions in depth and eventually settled on the path of yoga—the actual original Vedic tradition based on mantras, breathing practices, and meditations, which is at least three-thousand years old. I studied under several teachers (primarily Dr David Frawley), travelled to India, translated ancient Sanskrit texts, and developed familiarity with associated Vedic systems of knowledge, including Ayurveda, Jyotisha, and Vastu. I would often devote 4-6 hours a day practising yoga, and taught it for a number of years.

Did I come to understand consciousness? Did I find an answer to the ultimate question, Who am I? This was my quest at the time. Yes I did. There is a point of stillness reached in meditation that is the beginning of steady focus, which leads to deepening absorption in pure awareness. All other practices in yoga are simply to facilitate this state, known as *samādhi*. This is the real purpose of yoga—it's not simply stretching. In practising meditation, I came to experience my own consciousness directly. I will not say I completed this path, as those ancient mountains are vast and deep, and life is an ongoing river.

Instead, I started to think about how I was not Indian. Yes, that may seem an obvious point. But in the context of my journey, it was foundational. Yoga is an Indian (Hindu) tradition. Without going too much into the philosophy behind this, understanding the difference between pure consciousness (as formless awareness—what we might call spirit) and embodied consciousness (where consciousness is intrinsic to a specific identity—what we might call a soul) led me to want to understand my own ancestral heritage, both ancient and contemporary. I was not destined to remain a yogi, meditating on eternity in the forest. That was not who I was in this life.

Prior to five generations of Australians, my ancestors originate from north-western Europe, mainly English, Scottish, and Scandinavian. I explored my ancestral culture, history, places, traditions, practices, literature, language, art, and philosophy.

I did formal study in art history then completed my doctorate in English. I had scaled the transcendent mountains of consciousness through Eastern wisdom and was now to descend into the immanent valleys of my own Western heritage.

Writing was always a core part of my yoga work, as was reading, research, and teaching. These practices continued through the Western tradition; reading and writing poetry and fiction, academic research, teaching English to university students. I explored the creative, intellectual, practical, and spiritual elements of writing. Whether through Eastern or Western alchemical paths, my big dream has always been the quest for self-realisation and the actualisation of my full potential.

Awareness is central to this quest. I came to understand awareness as the primordial factor that not only determines our very existence, but brings everything in life into uniquely meaningful focus. While awareness provides a foundation and focus to being, I also believe it is important to apply oneself to mastering something specific and concrete in the world. For myself, this is writing.

It has been important for me to understand the various stages of my journey through life and how these are connected. While I may have left behind an opportunity to be a scientist, I still apply related elements in my life: in the more technical aspects of my work, data analysis, web design, exploring sacred geometry, or an interest in the lives of great entrepreneur-inventors of the past. There are always common threads, those recurring or rhyming themes in life.

Entrepreneurship is another element that has supported the different stages of my journey. I have developed several businesses, first as a yoga teacher, then a freelance writer, editor, artist, and designer, and more recently with my company, Genius Authoring. Having one's own business is one of the best ways to learn, grow, and help others as you pursue your own dreams.

So my journey has been inspired by some big dreams. The common thread of them all has been realising greater human potential through knowledge and creativity. Some dreams were met, some were stepping stones, and others were not to be. One way I look at my big dreams is to recognise the underlying question—and quest—that drove me toward each one. I have found that when my curiosity and calling were clear, it brought great energy, drive, interest, and a strong sense of why what I was doing was important.

To put it simply, I followed my inquisitiveness above all else. I started with wanting to understand how the universe operated—mainly through science. However, not being satisfied with scientific responses to the questions of who we are and why we are, I left this dream to be a scientist.

My questions spurred a deeper quest into meditation, spiritual traditions, transformative practices, philosophy, and culture. This was a life changing journey. My big dream was to attain self-realisation. In some ways, I arrived at this goal, but the journey is infinite and my soul was calling me in other directions.

I turned my quest for transformation toward more worldly applications by focusing on academic and then professional work as a writer. I founded my own company around writing and human potential. My dream entered into new settings and continues to grow.

My journey has been both continuous and evolving. Looking back, I can see how my steps tended to recur or rhyme with one another, orbiting around my desire to do something big—to realise my great dream. They continue to this day. Each stage of my journey prepared me for the next. Not every step seemed right at the time, but in the longer perspective, each step has been an integral contributor to who and where I am today.

I therefore value immensely the meaning and purpose one generates from recognising and working toward one's own unique big dream. Such dreams are not only highly likely to be the thing that sings most deeply in your heart, but also be of benefit to others—those close to you, perhaps even the wider world.

It's fine if people don't have such dreams, or don't want to pursue them—that's one's own choice. But for those who have a dream and don't pursue it, they will most certainly feel a loss within as the years pass.

This book is designed as a practical aid in the realisation—the making real—of one's greater dreams. If you have a big dream, I encourage you to pursue it. That is why I have written this book. The work I have done over the past two and a half decades to realise my own greater dreams has led me to some extremely meaningful human experiences. All the effort I put in was absolutely worth it.

Ultimately, if you are working toward what is truly your calling, you will become most alive and most fully yourself, in a very satisfying way. Even among setbacks and failures, for these are bound to come, the experience of meaning and purpose will evoke life's richer quality. Pursuing such a purposeful life also ensures that when the time comes to move on, you have given life your best and will not settle on a bed of regrets.

So as you work through the activities in this book to clarify and develop your future, keep in mind your journey so far. Look for those patterns of recurrence and rhyme that are unique to your life. While we can't always predict where our true ambitions will take us, we can look at our own past to gain an intuitive sense of life's timeless blueprint for each one of us.

I've shared my own example here so that you as a reader can see how I've approached the challenge of finding my own purpose and realising my dreams. I still have much more of the road to travel. Of course everyone thinks differently, has different personality traits, circumstances, and approaches to life. Your path will be different, unique, something only you can walk. Understanding what is uniquely yours is an important first step in becoming clear about your bigger dreams.

So that's my story, and some of the background on why I've written this book. Although I don't know exactly what my future journey will bring, I do clearly know where I am going and what I want to achieve. That brings me satisfaction. And because I have spent many years meditating, learning, writing, and applying my self to my greater goals in life, I have a good sense of how to work with whatever may come my way.

While one cannot always control what comes, knowing where you are going ensures you will not be a rudderless boat at the mercy of the deep blue sea. Working with whatever comes is like tacking against a headwind to one's advantage; you get to where you want to go even if life seems to be against you. Sure, this takes tenacity, resilience, and skill, but it also builds these qualities.

If you are to achieve your greatest dreams in life, you're going to need these qualities, and many others. You're going to need to become a high agency person—someone who makes life happen, rather than sitting in place expecting it to come to you. This book will help you develop these foundations.

You have what it takes, so get ready.

A great adventure is about to begin.

Vision without action is a daydream.
Action without vision is a nightmare.

– Japanese proverb

Section 2
Write your vision

What is your big dream?

The purpose of this section is for you to become clear about your big dream, your innermost calling, your purpose in life. We will reach this gradually through a series of writing activities and personal reflection. The result will be a written vision statement.

What does this dream need to be? That's up to you. It's your life and your big dream. The activities that follow will provide you with guidance to make the process easier, and you can do them in your own time, be creative, and revisit them as you need.

There are a few points to consider about the nature of this dream.

Firstly, it should be *your* dream, not your parents', the government's, or your boss's dream; not your sibling's or friend's dream; not some random's idea on the internet, or anyone else's. It needs to call to you from within. Your dream may be shared—with your partner, your family, or an organisation or community, for example. But the key point is that it must be part of you, something that resonates deeply with who you truly are.

Secondly, your dream needs to be worthy of your best, something big, a great aim for your life. It needs to be the biggest thing within you that you've always wanted to achieve, dreamt of becoming, what you long for and know to be your true calling and purpose. At the least, it needs to be something beyond your average aims.

You can use this process to explore and clarify smaller dreams too. But before you do, ask yourself if you're aiming small because you're afraid to aim big. Perhaps you should challenge that.

Your dream should also be something good. No dreams for world domination, enslavement of humanity, destruction of the Earth, that kind of thing. If these are your dreams, you might want to seek qualified professional help.

Use common sense—this is not an invitation to philosophise the meaning of 'good'. A good dream could be simply good for yourself or your family; it could be good for the entire country or world. But do think about the consequences should your dream become reality—what would happen to yourself and others? Consider both the positive and negative sides to it. Could you live with the reality?

Thirdly, your dream needs to be realistic, meaning that with the appropriate resources, time, knowledge, skills, and so on (even if you don't have these yet), it is possible in the real world. By all means think big, aim for greatness, and exercise the fullness of your imagination, but make the end goal real. If your dream involves time-travel or cloning aliens, I'm not going to judge you (much) for it, but I would advise you to focus on something more pragmatic. The whole reason for having a dream is to manifest it in the actual world. It may start with imagination, abstraction, or theory, but it must be able to move into the concrete world. While the next sections will address how to make your dream concrete, whatever you envision needs to be actually possible in the real world.

Finally, clarifying your dream into a vision is an iterative process, meaning it takes time to form and may require repetition of the exercises. Your vision statement will evolve as you spend time on it. And you should spend time with it—continue working on it until it is crystal clear, until you know it is exactly what it should be. The clearer it becomes, the greater likelihood of its realisation.

Take your time with all this. Don't expect an instant flash of insight, an epiphany of some kind. That might happen, but any such experiences should only be a starting point. Writing your vision clearly is as much visionary as it is an exercise in writing. The aim is to write your vision in clear and concise words. This process requires creativity and spontaneity at points, but also thoughtfulness and personal reflection. And it should be addressed in the context of your current life circumstances and your talents, skills, interests, and character.

Now to summarise these points. It needs to your dream. It should be worthy of your best. It needs to be realistic. And it is an iterative process.

So let's begin with some questions to clarify what your big dream is all about. Approach this creatively—there are no wrong answers and your ideas will become clearer as you go.

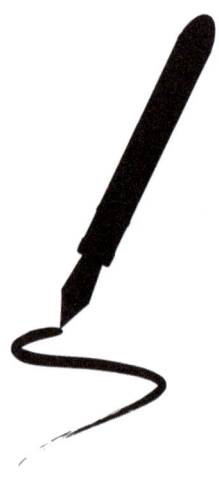

Create, explore, clarify

What is your biggest dream, your greatest ambition, your highest purpose or calling? Answer **spontaneously**; write whatever first comes to your mind without censoring yourself. Just try it.

_____
_____
_____
_____

What is the biggest thing you will regret not doing when you've reached the end of your life?

_____
_____
_____
_____

Next, if you had enough money that you didn't need to work for a living, and you had all the time in the world, what are the main activities you would do each day of the week? Write a short answer.

Monday: _____
Tuesday: _____
Wednesday: _____
Thursday: _____
Friday: _____
Saturday: _____
Sunday: _____

Read your answers from the previous page. What do they share in **common**? What is their **essence**? What in them reflects your big dream?

_____
_____
_____

Now, rewrite your biggest dream as a single sentence:

_____
_____
_____

While putting your dream into one sentence may be difficult, work at it as it will enable you to become clear about what you are aiming for.

Take a look at your single-sentence statement above. Read it aloud and observe **your own reaction** to each word.

What is it about this statement that **inspires** you most, and why?

_____
_____
_____
_____

If you find your statement uninspiring, you may want to return to the start of these questions and write the answers afresh.

Or, give yourself some space from the activity. Go for a short walk; do something else for a short time. Don't force an answer, but allow your mind to wander naturally. When the time is right, return to these questions and re-answer them.

Ready to continue? Examine your single-sentence statement from the previous page—**your vision statement**. What is unclear about it? What are you least sure about?

_____
_____

What words could you tweak (think of synonyms) to make your statement clearer and more aligned to your highest purpose in life? Rewrite your adjusted vision statement.

_____
_____

Is this revised vision statement missing anything? If so, what?

_____
_____

Rewrite your vision statement, updating it accordingly.

_____
_____
_____

Are you happy with this? If not, why not?

_____
_____

One final revision—rewrite your updated **vision statement**.

┌───┐
│   │
│   │
│   │
└───┘

We will build upon this statement in the coming sections.

The powerhouse of why

> He who has a *why?* in life
> can tolerate almost any *how?*
>
> – Friedrich Nietzsche

Nietzsche's quote is popular within motivated circles. If there's a solid **why** behind your big dream, it will keep you going. It will strengthen your resolve during setbacks and reveal itself in satisfying successes.

Your why is the powerhouse that keeps you resilient amid difficulties and focused amid victories. The key is to find the fundamental, most meaningful reason that underlies your big dream.

Why is your ultimate goal important?

Let's play the why game. Keep asking why about something to get to its root. Here's an example:

Why do I want to build a successful company? Because I want to do meaningful work aligned with my life's purpose.

Why? I value the time and effort I put into my work.

Why? I value myself.

Why? I believe I can contribute something valuable to others.

Why? I have put effort into self-development and accumulating knowledge and want to build something that is valuable to others.

Why? I care about the world I live in.

The important point is not only the final answer you arrive at, but also the exploration involved in getting to that.

It's also important to give a solid answer. This means moving toward what is real and genuine. You should be able to feel if your response is on target. There's an art to answering why.

You may end up going round in vacuous circles if you're not careful. If this happens, start your again from a different angle.

In the questions that follow, be creative while aiming to work toward the core reason behind your ultimate dream. Do the exercise several times if needed. Explore different possibilities, and spend some time reflecting on your answers.

Let's refresh what you wrote earlier. Write your vision statement from the previous page. **2**

_____

Why is this important? _____
_____

Why? _____
_____

Why? _____
_____

Why? _____
_____

Why? _____
_____

Let that final answer as to why on the previous page settle for a minute.

Drawing from the why-answers on the previous page, and adding your own thoughts, list the **top five reasons** why your ultimate goal is important.

1. _____
2. _____
3. _____
4. _____
5. _____

Do these reasons support the significance of your goal? If it really is a big and important goal for you, then your reasons should justify it. If they don't, you should return to the why-game activity on the previous page.

So, what's your conclusion—why does your ultimate goal matter? Write a few sentences.

_____
_____
_____
_____
_____

Summarise this in one sentence—we will call this your **why statement**.

Unpacking your ultimate dream

My **vision statement**:

My **why statement**:

Let's unpack things further. For each word below, write a short phrase that relates to your vision statement. The aim here is to expand both the ideas and the language around your vision statement and to think about your vision statement from a range of different angles. It's about associations.

There are no right or wrong answers. Write whatever comes to mind about your vision statement.

Energy _____

Time _____

Value _____

Cost _____

Problem _____

Solution _____

People _____

Skills _____

(This exercise continues on the next page.)

(Continue to unpack each word below.)

Knowledge _____

Essential _____

Excludes _____

Ideal _____

Sacrifice _____

Surface _____

Depth _____

Now _____

Later _____

Branches _____

Root _____

Fruit _____

These keywords are designed to evoke thought. What you do with these phrases in relation to the keywords is up to you. The main purpose of this exercise is to expand your range of ideas and vocabulary around your ultimate dream.

EIGHT QUESTIONS

You have a **why** statement. See if you can answer the following questions around your vision. There are a variety of ways to interpret each question, with no right or wrong answers. They are designed to stretch your thinking, so be creative.

Who? _____

_____

What? _____

_____

When? _____

Where? _____

Which? _____

Whence*? _____

Whither*? _____

How? _____

* Whence = from where. Whither = to where.

REFLECTION POINT

Well done making it this far! By now you should have a clear vision statement and a clear sense of why this is important. You should also have some surrounding ideas and language related to your vision and an early sense of how your vision orientates with the world. It doesn't need to be complete or perfect yet.

Now, let all this settle for an hour, a day, or a week. During this time, ask yourself: **Is this the greatest dream I have?**

Let your subconscious do the work here—don't stew on the question. Come back to it after this break and see how you feel about the answer. If the answer is 'no', you may want to start this section again, to become clearer about what you really want to do in your life.

Section 3
Form your goals

Concrete, achievable steps

When you look at a car, you see the finished product. But do you see all the steps that came together to bring it about? Not only the mechanical construction and assembly of many individual parts—a car is much more complex than this.

A completed car requires an engineering design process and plans, prototypes, and testing; computer coding and software integration; adherence to legal and safety regulations; logistics and supply chain management; factory cleaning and maintenance; marketing and sales campaigns; showrooms; customer service and repairs; all the people behind all these elements; the management and business administration to support those people; company financial management; shares and shareholder satisfaction; a board of directors, and so on. A car is a very complex, highly coordinated coalescence.

A car is a marvellous human achievement, and if it drives effortlessly for you it is only because of all the complexity and layers of work that have gone into making it this way. Moving from an idea to an actuality involved very specific, clearly-defined management strategy and design processes. It did not happen by chance.

Producing a car is one example of how complexity is orchestrated, how a process is refined and perfected, how something difficult is achieved. And the more difficult a goal, the more is required to make it a success.

The way to achieve a goal depends on what that goal is, the circumstances under which it is being pursued, and the people involved in pursuing it. There is no magic method or formula for achieving goals, yet there are ample techniques, tools, and methodologies—some new, some hype, some sound and well established—which may or may not be suitable for achieving your goal.

Furthermore, even the best tools require a human element for their effective application. Applying judgement, intelligence, resilience, conscientiousness, specific skills and knowledge, among other human qualities.

In short, achieving a goal requires many things and the journey toward it is unique. Your big dream is exactly this, so keep the practical realities of your dream in mind as you proceed.

In this section, we will take your vision statement from the previous section and develop some concrete, achievable steps toward making it real.

To achieve this, let's begin at the destination.

IMAGINE THE REALITY OF ACHIEVING YOUR BIG DREAM

Find a place and time where you won't be disturbed for 10-15 minutes. Put your phone aside and on silent. Find a comfortable seat and close your eyes.

Picture yourself after having achieved your big dream. You've done it! It's actually real.

How does it feel?

Who else is involved and how do they feel about it?

What new things happen as a result? What changes does it bring?

Picture the specific details. Imagine the colours, sounds, smells, tastes, and textures.

Imagine the thoughts and feelings you experience.

What does a typical day involve for you?

Picture other people's facial expressions, hear their words.

What they are doing in relation to this achievement?

How does your achievement affect the wider world?

What does your life look like? What are the concrete and practical realities?

4 Once you've spent some time picturing this, open your eyes and write this experience below. Describe what you imagine happening, having achieved your dream. Emphasise the concrete outcomes. Write in short sentences or dot points.

_____
_____
_____
_____
_____
_____
_____
_____
_____
_____
_____
_____
_____

Once you've finished, read what you've written.

The obstacles make it real

*The astute mind sees
the potential in the actual.*

*Every challenge is an opportunity.
Every obstacle a transformative gateway.
Every unknown a pool of knowledge.*

Having a big dream is a truly great thing, but it remains mere fantasy as long as one is not realistic toward it. One way to become realistic about it is to focus on the problems involved in reaching it, address the obstacles, face the hard realities. Those who avoid looking at the difficult aspects of their dream are almost certainly going to come up against them unprepared, and therefore be far less likely to succeed in achieving their dream. It's one thing to have an amazing vision but it's another to make it a reality. And that's what we are here for.

To think one can reach a goal without addressing the problems involved with it is wishful thinking. Some people might be easily motivated by the rewards of a goal, whether those along the way or at the end. But these rewards are intrinsically connected to the obstacles that prevent one reaching them. In a way, the obstacles encapsulate the potential reward. Therefore, the more you can recognise that by overcoming obstacles you are rewarded, you can shift your focus from seeking reward to solving problems.

If you can learn to love the challenges more than the rewards, you will remain practical toward achieving your goal and will become unstoppable in your motivation.

Loving the overcoming of obstacles also shifts the focus from simply getting to the destination to actually experiencing (and enjoying) the journey. I know, "it's about the journey not the destination" is an overdone metaphor, but it's supported by psychology, as was mentioned in the Introduction. There is great satisfaction and meaning in pursuing a challenging purpose.

At the same time, your great dream will most likely be something that is genuinely valuable for yourself and others. So while pursing this may be very difficult at times, both the process and the outcome are valuable.

In any case, you will need the right mindset when facing obstacles as you work toward your vision. This means being honest about the difficulties involved, as well as the realities of what's required to overcome them.

Let's explore this further.

5. CHALLENGES

In the previous section, you listed the top five reasons why your vision statement is important. Now consider the five biggest problems, obstacles, or challenges you are likely to face in making this vision a reality. These could be at any stage of progress toward your vision. Write these down.

1. _____
2. _____
3. _____
4. _____
5. _____

RESOURCES

6

What resources does each of these challenges require for you to overcome them? Resources could include both material and immaterial things—such as time, money, specific skills or knowledge, character traits, particular people, physical things, certain circumstances etc. Be specific and practical.

For example, perhaps you need a visa so you can work in a foreign country. In this case you would list this, and might also include the visa duration, the approximate cost, and the sponsor name.

Don't go into too much detail—that will come later when you act on your plan. The aim here is to be realistic about the challenges and what they require. You may not have these resources yet—this will be addressed in coming activities. You may also decide that gaining such resources is in itself a challenge, so update your top challenges on the previous page accordingly.

List the resources required to overcome each of the top five challenges you've written on the previous page; include any significant and relevant details.

1. _____
   _____

2. _____
   _____

3. _____
   _____

4. _____
   _____

5. _____
   _____

Knowing what is reliable

As you move about in the world, things shift and change. Some goals can be really difficult, or a seemingly achievable goal can meet unexpected circumstances as it progresses. You're going to need to know what you can rely upon as you progress toward your dream. This may not be initially clear. You will undoubtably also encounter new elements along the way that prove reliable.

7 In the context of achieving your vision, list what elements you can presently rely upon—this may include a particular person, resource, skill, knowledge, character trait or principle, organisation, tool, book, place, song, belief, or anything else. Write what each can be relied upon for, and rate how reliable each is (1 being least; 10 being most). Try to complete the entire list, even if you're stretching it and some things are less reliable (which is also good to know). Be honest and realistic.

Element	Relied upon for?	Reliability
_____	_____	1 2 3 4 5 6 7 8 9 10
_____	_____	1 2 3 4 5 6 7 8 9 10
_____	_____	1 2 3 4 5 6 7 8 9 10
_____	_____	1 2 3 4 5 6 7 8 9 10
_____	_____	1 2 3 4 5 6 7 8 9 10
_____	_____	1 2 3 4 5 6 7 8 9 10
_____	_____	1 2 3 4 5 6 7 8 9 10
_____	_____	1 2 3 4 5 6 7 8 9 10
_____	_____	1 2 3 4 5 6 7 8 9 10
_____	_____	1 2 3 4 5 6 7 8 9 10

Look at how many of these elements belong to you and how many belong to other people. Those that belong to other people will be to some degree beyond your control.

If an element is owned by you, you may need to consider how accessible it is within your environment, and how durable it is over time.

If it is not owned by you, consider the cost or exchange necessary to access its reliability.

How might you use these reliable elements when facing the biggest challenges that you listed previously (on page 42)?

_____
_____
_____
_____
_____
_____

What can you do to strengthen the reliable elements that are required or will be helpful for achieving your vision?

_____
_____
_____
_____
_____
_____

Steps and milestones

Once you have a clear, realistic vision of what you are aiming for, we can apply a technique known as backward mapping.

Backward mapping involves breaking a big goal down into a series of smaller milestones and steps to achieve those. How exactly you break this down depends on the nature of the goal. This exercise works best when you make each step well defined and practically achievable. If the steps are too large, they may become overly complex and difficult. If they are too small, you can get lost in the details. This exercise will help you find the right size steps.

Make sure you consider the challenges, resources, and reliable elements that might be required (from the previous pages). Factor these into the steps. Once you're done, you should have a series of clearly defined and realistically achievable smaller goals that are steps and milestones leading to your ultimate end goal.

8 Summarise the destination of your vision—your **end goal**.

_____

Now map **three milestones** backwards from this end goal to where you are today. For example, if your end goal is to live in Italy, milestones might be: C—'move to Italy', B—'secure a job and accommodation', and A—'save money'. Have a few attempts if you need; create a clear outline of three roughly equal-sized stages.

- **End goal**
- **Milestone C** _____
- **Milestone B** _____
- **Milestone A** _____
- **Today**

Now do the same backward mapping, but this time include **twelve steps**. Use the three milestones you already have, spaced evenly among the twelve steps, for a total of fifteen.

These steps need to be specific, practical, and achievable smaller goals. They should consider the challenges that need to be overcome and the resources you will need to obtain. These steps need to lead back through the three milestones, ultimately to today.

- **End goal** _____
- **Step 12** _____
- **Step 11** _____
- **Step 10** _____
- **Milestone C** _____
- **Step 9** _____
- **Step 8** _____
- **Step 7** _____
- **Milestone B** _____
- **Step 6** _____
- **Step 5** _____
- **Step 4** _____
- **Milestone A** _____
- **Step 3** _____
- **Step 2** _____
- **Step 1** _____
- **Today**

This is your road to success! Your foundational **plan**.

Read your plan from today through to the end goal and see if everything feels right. If something is out of place, change it.

This is your road to travel and it needs to work for you.

A SHORT BREAK

Next, we're going to unpack this further. But before we move on, you might like to take a break.

In the next section we will closely analyse each step in your plan, so it's a bit more involved but will give you a clear understanding of the road to travel.

Navigation through analysis

To navigate toward your end goal requires understanding the conditions at each stage of the journey. By analysing each step and milestone on your plan, you will gain a better sense of the terrain and how to traverse it.

We will apply four factors for this analysis:

Solid—this is the factor in any given step or milestone that you can rely upon and build upon to progress to the next step or milestone.

Slippery—this is the factor in any given step or milestone that presents the most risk, which is most likely to prevent you from achieving that step or milestone and could even prevent the entire end goal from being achieved.

Costly—this is the factor in any given step or milestone that is going to require the most resources (of any kind—time, effort, money, knowledge etc.) to achieve that step or milestone.

Lucky—this is the beneficial factor of a given step or milestone that is outside of your control. If you can obtain it, however, it will make achieving that step or milestone much easier. There's no guarantee of it, but there may be ways to increase the chances of it coming about.

I recommend adopting a common-sense approach when considering each factor, including focusing on the most prominent single thing for each factor. A clear analysis of the most prominent single element will be much more useful in practice than building a complex, multi-element perspective. The purpose of this analysis is to reveal a clear understanding that informs successful action.

With the four factors in mind, **apply the process below** to fill out the quadrants on the following pages.

- Firstly, write the step or milestone at the top of each page.

- Then, in the box labelled **what** for each factor, name what each factor is for that step or milestone.

  For example, the solid factor for a step might be that you have expertise in an essential skill which that step needs, in which case you would add the name of that skill.

- Next, in the **power** box for each factor, estimate the influence—for good or ill—that this factor has over the step or milestone, ranging from 0 (powerless) to 10 (extremely strong).

  For example, your essential skill might have an influence of 8 out of 10, because you are quite capable in that area.

- Finally, fill out the other boxes in each quadrant.

  For the **solid** and **lucky** factors, write in a few words the **gift** (the positive contribution) that factor may bring to the step or milestone. Then write how you can best make **use** of this gift.

  For the **slippery** and **costly** factors, write in a few words the **challenge** (the requirement, the problem) that factor may bring to the step or milestone. Then write the **solution** to this challenge.

This activity takes some time, so pace yourself and persevere. Be logical, but also trust your instinct. How you approach this activity very much depends on the nature of each step or milestone and how each progresses toward your end goal.

Once you've completed this activity, you should have a much better understanding of each step and milestone, which will establish a strong foundation for success.

STEP 1 _____

Solid				Slippery	
Use					Solution
Gift					Challenge
What		Power	Power		What
What		Power	Power		What
Challenge					Gift
Solution					Use
Costly				Lucky	

Notes

STEP 2 _____

	Solid			Slippery	
Use					Solution
Gift					Challenge
What		Power	Power		What
What		Power	Power		What
Challenge					Gift
Solution					Use
	Costly			Lucky	

Notes

STEP 3 _____

Solid			Slippery	
Use				Solution
Gift				Challenge
What		Power	Power	What
What		Power	Power	What
Challenge				Gift
Solution				Use
Costly			Lucky	

Notes

MILESTONE A _____

	Solid			Slippery	
Use					Solution
Gift					Challenge
What		Power	Power		What
What		Power	Power		What
Challenge					Gift
Solution					Use
	Costly			Lucky	

Notes

STEP 4 _____

Solid				Slippery			
Use							Solution
Gift							Challenge
What			Power	Power			What
What			Power	Power			What
Challenge							Gift
Solution							Use
Costly				Lucky			

Notes

STEP 5 _____

	Solid			Slippery	
Use					Solution
Gift					Challenge
What		Power	Power		What
What		Power	Power		What
Challenge					Gift
Solution					Use
	Costly			Lucky	

Notes

STEP 6 _____

Solid				Slippery		
Use						Solution
Gift						Challenge
What		Power	Power			What
What		Power	Power			What
Challenge						Gift
Solution						Use
Costly				Lucky		

Notes

MILESTONE B _____

Solid		Slippery	
Use			Solution
Gift			Challenge
What	Power	Power	What
What	Power	Power	What
Challenge			Gift
Solution			Use
Costly		Lucky	

Notes

STEP 7 _____

Solid				Slippery	
Use					Solution
Gift					Challenge
What		Power	Power		What
What		Power	Power		What
Challenge					Gift
Solution					Use
Costly				Lucky	

Notes

STEP 8 _____

Solid				Slippery	
Use					Solution
Gift					Challenge
What		Power	Power		What
What		Power	Power		What
Challenge					Gift
Solution					Use
Costly				Lucky	

Notes

STEP 9 _____

	Solid			Slippery	
Use					Solution
Gift					Challenge
What		Power	Power		What
What		Power	Power		What
Challenge					Gift
Solution					Use
	Costly			Lucky	

Notes

MILESTONE C _____

Solid		Slippery	
Use			Solution
Gift			Challenge
What	Power	Power	What
What	Power	Power	What
Challenge			Gift
Solution			Use
Costly		Lucky	

Notes

64 | FORM YOUR GOALS

STEP 10 _____

Solid			Slippery	
USE				SOLUTION
GIFT				CHALLENGE
WHAT	POWER	POWER		WHAT
WHAT	POWER	POWER		WHAT
CHALLENGE				GIFT
SOLUTION				USE
Costly			Lucky	

Notes

STEP 11 _____

Solid			Slippery	
Use				Solution
Gift				Challenge
What		Power	Power	What
What		Power	Power	What
Challenge				Gift
Solution				Use
Costly			Lucky	

Notes

STEP 12 _____

Solid				Slippery	
Use					Solution
Gift					Challenge
What		Power	Power		What
What		Power	Power		What
Challenge					Gift
Solution					Use
Costly				Lucky	

Notes

FORM YOUR GOALS | 67

END GOAL _____

Solid				Slippery	
USE					SOLUTION
GIFT					CHALLENGE
WHAT		POWER	POWER		WHAT
WHAT		POWER	POWER		WHAT
CHALLENGE					GIFT
SOLUTION					USE
Costly				Lucky	

Notes

You should now have a detailed analysis of each step toward your end goal. As you approach each step, you can refer to this analysis as a map and allow it to guide how you approach that step.

Be aware that this map is not static. The steps you take and their factors and circumstances may change as you progress toward your goal. Therefore it is useful to revisit your steps periodically—at the completion of each milestone. A process for this will be outlined in the next section.

The end goal is included with an analysis quadrant because it is the final step in your road. Your analysis of this end goal will provide you with greater understanding of the nature of your goal.

Your analysis of the end goal will also show you its boundaries. Being clear about both what your goal is and what it is not is very useful, because this will allow you to better plan and prepare the road toward it.

Thinking outside the boundaries of your goal is also useful because your goal certainly doesn't exist in isolation from the wider world. Not considering those forces and influences that are outside of your goal but might still impact upon it is like buying a very nice house but not considering the money required for council rates, insurance, and repairs. The result is that you get the house but can't maintain it. Your goal is centrally important, but is nonetheless placed within a very complex, larger world. Keep it in perspective.

In summary, aim to maintain a broad perspective around your end goal, have a clear sense of its boundaries, and focus on its centre: what you are working toward.

Let's clarify some of these aspects.

What is your end goal (from the previous page)?

_____

_____

What are the boundaries of your goal? What is it not?

_____

_____

_____

_____

_____

What are the significant factors outside of your end goal that might influence it?

_____

_____

_____

_____

_____

REFLECTION POINT

Getting to this point has likely required a lot of thought and effort on your part. Now you deserve a break. Let your unconscious mind to do its side of the work for a while.

Spend some time with people close to you, get some exercise in nature, do something you enjoy that's relaxing. Allow the work you've done in this section to settle for a day, or several. Be precise as to when you will return, and stick to it. Mark that date and time in your calendar.

See you in the next section!

Section 4
Prepare for action

The art of turning dreams into reality

This section is all about action. But I'm not going to tell you what you should do—that is up to you. Instead, what follows are a series of perspectives, guidance, activities, and tools to prepare you for action and support you in achieving your steps, milestones, and end goal.

There is no right way to use these, so be creative and exercise your initiative. You may find some particularly useful when you are facing difficulties or obstacles in the path toward your dream. Refer to them as you need.

There can be many paths of action toward an intended step or milestone, and this action occurs within complex and changing environments. As you progress, you may need to adjust your approach, try several different ways, or hold back on a particular action while you gain more knowledge or skill in that area. Hence, of the three levels of this book (writing your vision, forming your goals, and planning your actions), this section on action is the most dynamic, spontaneous, and flexible—as it should be.

The other two levels are less mercurial. The goals you form (steps and milestones) should not be readily changed, unless they are not working and need adjustment. And, to the degree that your vision is true to your greatest dreams, you should keep it fixed. Your vision is your true north star that will guide you through all the vicissitudes of the world. It provides a constant which you can advance toward through clearly defined goals, which are achieved by dynamic, intelligent action.

We can therefore consider these three levels as fixed (vision), developing (goals), and dynamic (action). Your vision is unmoving, your goals adapt and adjust only as required to ensure the vision is reached, and your action is entirely free and flexible as is necessary to reach your steps, milestones, and end goal.

I DREAM, I PLAN, AND I ACT, THEREFORE I AM

To receive something valuable through the great generosity of another can be a great joy. For example, imagine you inherent five million dollars from an uncle, through no effort of your own.

But would you truly value it? Studies estimate that for wealthy families passing down an inheritance, 70% will lose their wealth by the second generation, 90% by the third generation.[5]

However, it is an entirely different game to make that five million through your own hard work, resolve, and resilience over several years. Earning something that way ensures that you truly value it.

More importantly, earning something changes *you* in the process—in the beginning you did not qualify for it and had you received it you would not likely relate to it in the same way as you would if you had worked, solved problems, and pushed against obstacles in order to gain it.

Gifts are certainly good. But the valuable results from your own deliberate actions are far better—having more intrinsic substance, depth, and personal meaning. You then confirm what you are capable of, and that confidence, knowledge, and ability become part of you and will remain with you even if you lose everything you gained externally.

In the same way, realising your dreams through your own planning and action makes them truly yours. Achieving your big dream means that you have become what was of innermost value to you. You live as your true self within the world.

The real essence of turning dreams into reality is not the results of your actions. It is how you transform as a result. You become the dreamer, the creator, the person with the qualities, knowledge, and skills through which to make dreams a reality. You come to master the art of making real your soul's vision.

Such transformation is far more powerful and permanent than any material inheritance, even while wealth is useful for doing great things. By transforming yourself, you become the centre of your own power to enact positive transformation. This not only enables you to use wealth wisely, but also to be a generator of wealth.

Don't become a slave to your attainments and successes, let alone your failures or losses. Keep your centre within yourself and become a more complete, integrated human being.

EVERYTHING'S ON A PLATTER, BUT THE BEST FOOD IS WITHIN

We live in an age where at the push of a button, food of your choice is delivered to your door. While technology is at our fingertips, you will not receive your big dream at your doorstep because the world does not have as its priority your deepest satisfaction.

Selling and influencing are everywhere, not only in the information we receive but in the very mediums through which that information is conveyed. Systems are designed, constrained, filtered, measured, and carefully orchestrated so that you become a superficial product serving another's gains.

While these systems are often voluntary on our part, and we do gain something from using them, their structure consists of layers of artificial environments whose rules we do not, and cannot, alter. It is one thing to live in a universe whose laws of nature apply equally to all and allow for ingenuity, creative freedom, and concrete unbiased feedback. It is another to live in someone else's construct.

Paradigms and worldviews within politics, religion, and philosophy have for millennia set up such frameworks to sway the human masses. And today not much has changed. We often subject ourselves to other's paradigms unwittingly and voluntarily. We become confined to these to the degree we do not exercise our consciousness.

This is because consciousness is different from and deeper than all paradigms—even while containing them. Consciousness is the witnessing power of innate awareness. It always presents a degree of freedom regardless of the circumstances. Learning to exercise one's potential consciousness is an essential gateway to mastery.

As you work through this book you can learn to develop the art of turning dreams into realities. Exercising this art can produce results ranging from minor outcomes to something immense. However, it's important to uncover what is truly yours to build into a reality, rather than adopting what the world thinks you need. If you've worked with the earlier sections of this book, your unique dream and the steps to get there should be clear to you. Now it's time for action.

SELF-DETERMINATION IS BAKED INTO THE CAKE

Even if you do find the tools in this book useful, there will be points at which you will need to go in your own direction, off the track so to speak. Like any art, the art of turning dreams into realities has a variety of techniques, people, and other resources available from which learn and gather experience.

But there are also times in which initiative and innovation are essential—as well as other traits like courage, discernment, wisdom, and patience. As you progress you become more self-reliant through developing such qualities. Working it out for yourself becomes second-nature.

Mastering the art of turning dreams into reality is as much about knowing the nature of reality as it is dreaming clearly. You must be both very pragmatic and very imaginative. We all yearn to make our dreams come true, but most people tend to drown them out through distractions and unclear internal consciousness. The art of turning dreams into reality requires the development of self-awareness as much as it requires pragmatic mastery in the world. You need to become both a dreamer and an achiever, a visionary and a realist.

Developing this art, like any art, requires practice and experience. It's certainly not theory. You need to work at envisioning your goals and doing what is necessary to successfully realise them—for big and small goals alike. Becoming highly skilled at this art makes you an unstoppable force in the world, while allowing you to realise your unique purpose in life through fulfilment of those dreams that resonate most deeply within the core of your being. This is no small thing; neither is it necessarily easy.

This book focuses on helping you achieve one of your big dreams. But this one dream is merely the beginning of something much greater—namely, gaining proficiency in the art herein mentioned, which combines envisioning lofty goals, forming plans, and mastering action.

The last of these three, action, is by far the most difficult, which is why some people remain forever dreamers or planners, seeing what they want and thinking about it, but failing to make it real.

Therefore, in the spirit of practice as the best way to learn any art, let's continue working toward your big dream by looking at some of the elements involved in mastering action.

CONSCIOUS ACTION

The best action is conscious action.

Simply put, conscious action is being aware of what you're doing, while you're doing it. There are a number of ways to approach this. Here are some you can try:

Practise self-awareness: When you act, watch yourself like an observer; watch your body, physical movements, breathing, emotions, thoughts, feelings and sensations. Observe yourself in action so that you can be aware of how your entire being is responding to the actions you undertake.

This is a practice of heightened awareness and focused absorption. It will enable you to act more deliberately and effectively, with self-discipline, helping you stay on track with your plan and reducing the likelihood of reacting thoughtlessly to situations (which could result in actions contrary to your plan). It will also enable you to better enjoy the action in and of itself.

Eyes on the prize: Keep your greatest dream in your heart. If this is truly your deepest, most important and meaningful goal in life, then remembering this in your heart will provide you with a limitless determination and wellspring of energy. As you act, especially when you face great challenges, recall why you are doing this. Feel your big dream in your heart and allow that to power you toward it.

Peel away distractions and counter wrong turns: To get to your goal, you're going to need to minimise those elements of your life that run counter to it. These could be internal or external. Sometimes they are strong and may seem impossible to avoid. But you must work on overcoming such things. Being self-aware and aware of your actions is one method to rise above the subconscious tendencies that may pull you in other directions.

Deliberate conscious action means saying to yourself, "Now I will do [x]" then doing it as best as you can, consistently and consciously, until it is complete. Of course, when acting on a large task, you will need to break it up into manageable chunks.

While you act, if something else arises, if you are distracted by other things, if you take a wrong turn and end up wasting time on pointless things that won't bring your dream closer to reality, then consider what really matters. Consider the limited time you have in this life and what you cannot afford to miss out on.

While sufficient rest, relaxation, and recuperation can make you more effective during the time that you're working on your goal, no amount of time wasting and distraction is going to bring about your ultimate goal. Neither will diversions be as rewarding. Forget the diversions. Get good sleep, eat well, take care of yourself and those around you, and work hard toward your goal. Exercise your discipline and you will be rewarded, both now and in the future.

POWERFUL PURPOSEFUL ACTION

Action requires specific skills, traits and knowledge. Master those skills, traits, or knowledge that are required to meet your goal. Learn and improve them as you act.

Action requires clarity and understanding. Looking backward, reflect and learn from the results of what you do. Looking forward, understand the landscape and clearly envision your target. The world is both potential and actual. Adapt your thinking to creative possibilities while making your action practical and decisive. Dream your goals into being through wise and bold pragmatic action.

Additional important factors for effective action include principles, practices, observation and timing, opportunistic spontaneity, scope and purpose, and rhythm and recurrence. Let's explore these.

Principles: Principles are the enduring values that will empower you to best achieve your end goal through a course of action. They shape *how* you go about successfully moving from where you are now to the next step or milestone. They are not your plan (that is your *what*), although any plan should be aligned with your principles. Some examples of principles include patience, boldness, kindness, and respect. Strong principles will support you in the face of difficult situations because they transcend the particulars of any situation. They will give you the best chance of success because they are aligned to your core, which is your true source of strength.

Refresh yourself on your vision statement. What are the core principles that will support you to achieve your big dream? **11**

_____

_____

_____

Practices: In contrast to principles, practices are more immediate forms of action. They are the core disciplines, skills, and applied knowledge that contribute toward you achieving your end goal. Some examples are writing (for the goal of becoming a renown author), building (for building one's own home), or logistics (for creating an import/export company).

Practices should be built into your daily training, developed through experience, and mastered over time. You should seek to continually improve in them, across any and all circumstances, in a creative and intelligent manner. You can test your limits with them by challenging yourself slightly beyond your assumed capability, to expand your potential. Practices take into account the environment, circumstances, people, and everything else involved. They work best when integrated with your principles. While principles are the spirit of action, practices are the body.

12 What are the most important practices you will need to master in order to be successful in achieving your end goal?

_____

_____

_____

Include in your daily or weekly routine time to train and develop these practices. You can also seek out additional resources that expand your knowledge of them, be it books, videos, instructors, training partners, and so on. As you master them, you will greatly increase your success in advancing toward your end goal.

Observation and timing: The ability to observe an environment or scenario is crucial to understanding how to best act within it. Observation brings direct knowledge, which will enhance your effectiveness in acting. Furthermore, as you observe people, patterns, rhythms, and cycles, you will come to understand how to apply timely action.

Spend some time patiently observing an environment or situation that is relevant to your goals. Develop your ability in observation. Consider how your plans, principles, and practices can best be applied to the environment or situation.

Learn to become a strategic observer by being alert to the optimal time for particular actions. Practice observation when you need time to reflect, are seeking to understand the best way forward, or when you become stuck.

Opportunistic spontaneity: Powerful action takes advantage of opportunities that arise. Opportunistic spontaneity is about acting swiftly at the optimal time that an opportunity presents itself. A degree of calculated risk should be present in such spontaneity, as one needs to learn to rapidly assess any situation as to whether a spontaneous response is worth the risk.

As you go about your actions, be alert to the opportunities that arise and how quickly, confidently, and effectively you respond to them. Consider the following questions:

Are you risk adverse or risk inclined? _____

Are you good at calculating risk? _____

Do you follow through with action whose reward is proportionate to the risk? _____

How might you adopt a more balanced approach to risk?

_____

_____

_____

_____

Various factors contribute to a strong foundation for exercising opportunistic spontaneity, including knowing who you are and what you are capable of, understanding human nature and a range of environments, courage and boldness, a fall-back plan, and being generally prepared for anything life will throw at you.

Scope and purpose: In any given scenario, you could act in a variety of ways to achieve an outcome. There are no doubt actions you wouldn't think of, as well as actions you may not want to do due to them being outside of your comfort zone (even though you might get the result you need—I'm not referring to immoral or harmful action, which should be avoided). Sometimes it's necessary to re-evaluate the scope of your thinking, particularly if you are stuck. Be flexible.

At the same time, the scope of your action should be balanced by a sharp focus and strategic prioritisation.

14 As you work on each step or milestone, ask yourself: What possibilities are there? What is the most effective course of action? Apply yourself to those actions that are aligned to your purpose and most likely to achieve your next step or milestone.

How thoroughly have you considered the possible ways forward? And how many of these are truly worthwhile, on track to your purpose and worth the risk? Write about the possible actions from your current position.

_____

_____

_____

_____

_____

You can revisit this activity anytime you feel stuck and unclear about the next best course of action.

Rhythm and recurrence: Energy is built through momentum, which comes from recurring rhythmic action. Your big dream is a marathon, not a sprint.

Ocean waves can wear away stone over time. Therefore, as you develop the best ways to act in order to achieve your goals, you also need to repeat these actions steadily and purposefully in order to build momentum. Interweave recuperation within your rhythm. This means having a break and doing something to recharge at regular times. Avoid unwholesome recreational activities that numb your mind and drain your energy. Instead, nourish yourself during your down-time. Seek sources of inspiration and energy to enhance your success, including uplifting people, nature, books or other media, or experiences that will quicken you toward your goals.

Write a paragraph describing the rhythms of your action and recuperation. **15**

_____
_____
_____
_____
_____

Write down how might you adopt a more balanced approach to rest?

_____
_____
_____

List some sources of inspiration and energy you can access during recreation or recuperation time?

_____
_____
_____
_____

Initially, try to explore a wide range of sources. As you develop your momentum and experience, you will find which ones work best. Keep a balance between being open to new experiences and engaged with what works best for you.

What you do is as important as what you don't do. Be wise in your choices, so that you're not driving with the handbrake on—making your journey harder than it needs to be.

Recalibrate at the milestones

As you progress on the road toward your end goal, circumstances can change. For this reason, when you reach a milestone you should consider whether you need to recalibrate your analysis of the upcoming steps. Here is a process for doing this. It is also an opportunity to learn from what you've done.

THE RECALIBRATION PROCESS

When you complete a milestone, consider the following:

1. Look at your achievement and congratulate yourself for having reached it. You may have an ideal result or it may not have turned out exactly as you planned. Never mind that for now. Firstly, celebrate the good that you've achieved. Mark the occasion with something special—a dinner with those involved, a visit to a special place, a weekend away—choose whatever you think suitable.

2. Next, reflect on what you've done. Look at each of the three prior steps and note (in the section below each quadrant):

    a. what went well

    b. what didn't go well

    c. what you learnt from completing this milestone.

3. Finally, look at the next three steps to come (page 47) and the analysis quadrants you prepared for each of these steps (pages 52-67). For each step ask:

    Does this step need adjusting or fine-tuning, given where I am now, to keep me on track and able to reach the end goal most effectively?

Make any changes you see are needed for that step, then move to the next step and repeat, until you reach the next milestone (or end goal if you're at the final milestone).

4. Examine your recalibrated steps. Check that they remain on track toward the next milestone and end goal. Make sure any changes you've made are an improvement and that they will better facilitate you reaching the next milestone and end goal.

Use the table below to map any major changes.

End goal

Step 12

Step 11

Step 10

Milestone C

Step 9

Step 8

Step 7

Milestone B

Step 6

Step 5

Step 4

Milestone A

Step 3

Step 2

Step 1

BEFORE AFTER

You're going to want to quit

Anyone who's ever done anything difficult before (and who hasn't) would have experienced the feeling of wanting to give up. If you haven't, perhaps you haven't gone far enough.

A bigger challenge, more difficult, more costly, taking longer, multiple obstacles, more discouragement, unexpected injuries or losses—all these factors multiply that feeling.

Despair not. There is abundant guidance from those who have walked toward their highest destiny.

"There is no easy way from the earth to the stars." – Seneca

"Our greatest weakness lies in giving up. The most certain way to succeed is always to try just one more time." – Thomas Edison

"I am not concerned that you have fallen—I am concerned that you arise." – Abraham Lincoln

It is not those who fail that never achieve their dreams, but those who never learn from their failure and never give it another go with greater wisdom, knowledge, and determination.

If you're about to quit, read a biography of someone who inspires, who is a great example. Such people have risen triumphantly to greatness despite all obstacles. And they are just as human as you are, so you've always got a chance.

It doesn't mean they're invincible and it certainly doesn't mean they didn't feel like quitting at some point. But quitting is only a temporary solution. Your dream will remain, waiting for you, calling to you from within to reap its rewards.

At these darkest moments of wanting to quit, take a break and do something for your own self-development. This might be going for a walk in nature, exercise, a good meal, or spending some time with positive, uplifting people.

If this isn't enough to settle your mind's misgivings and reignite your soul, there may be deeper conflicts within that you need to resolve. Take a bit more time out. Spend that time learning a course, a language, a musical instrument; develop a new skill; participate in a community; travel. In doing these things, you are not giving up. It's a hiatus, a pause to give yourself time and space to reflect upon how far you have come, what really matters to you, and the nature of the obstacles you presently face.

Nothing of value ever came easily. The quitting obstacle is the perfect opponent by which you can reinforce your reasons for resolve, strengthen your strategies, and transform yourself for tomorrow.

FAILURE IS AN UNAVOIDABLE ASPECT OF SUCCESS

Too often we are taught that failure is irreversible; that it is an indication one is not made for that path and should choose differently. This may be valid when you are not particularly interested in that path. But where you are truly passionate and deeply interested, you should not give your dream up so easily.

There are numerous stories of successful people throughout history who started out from a difficult place and faced immense setbacks, rejections, disparagement, and other obstacles as they strove to reach their dream. For such people, failure was not the end, but an opportunity to learn, improve, and reapply oneself with greater determination.

If you were already perfect, you would never fail. Learning from failure and persevering is a true sign of your inevitable success.

Imagine your wiser self into action

Here's an exercise to help you tap into your own wisdom. You can use it any time.

This exercise involves having an imaginary conversation with your older, wiser, very astute and experienced 95 year-old self. (If you're older than 95, congratulations—pick someone you consider wise and able to give you good, practical advice.)

You can do this exercise lying in bed or sitting with eyes closed as a meditation. Or you can do it as a journalling exercise, where you write a dialogue between yourself and your 95-year-old self.

Begin by imagining yourself somewhere with your older, wiser self. Tell your older self the situation you are experiencing, the challenges, successes, and problems. Listen to what they say in response. Spend time conversing with them within your imagination. Once you're finished, thank your wiser, older self for their guidance.

Don't trip yourself up with the question of whether what you're imagining is real or not—that's irrelevant. What's important here is the advice and guidance that your mind imagines. Suspend disbelief. It's an activity in creative imagination, which helps you tap into your unconscious mind.

If you're journalling this activity, take your time writing down what comes to you. Allow your pen to write whatever comes without thinking about it—get it on the page.

If you're doing the activity purely in your imagination, take some notes of the main points afterwards.

There are two learning opportunities in this activity. The first is from examining how you described your situation and challenges. The second is in the guidance you receive from your wiser self.

How did you describe your situation and challenges to your wiser self?

_____
_____
_____
_____
_____
_____

What guidance did you receive from your wiser self?

_____
_____
_____
_____
_____
_____

Reflect upon both facets in order to better understand how you might proceed from here.

One's own self can be the biggest obstacle and the greatest power.

By examining both facets, you are positioning yourself outside of any current difficulties in order to gain a new perspective on those difficulties. This helps you gain a more objective point of view. You are also tapping into the wisdom of your unconscious through your imagination. Examining both facets with objective discernment can help you refine your understanding of your own conscious perspective.

HOW WOULD YOU ADVISE YOUR BEST FRIEND?

This exercise is a variant on the previous one.

Suppose your best friend was in your current situation, experiencing the exact challenges and problems that you are currently facing as you work toward achieving your end goal. What would you say to them? What advice would you give?

As in the previous exercise, play out this scenario in your imagination, or write it down. Once you're done, reflect on the words of advice you shared.

18 What did you imagine yourself saying to your best friend?

_____
_____
_____
_____
_____

How did you imagine your best friend responded?

_____
_____
_____
_____
_____

Reflect upon both facets in order to better understand how to best move forward.

As with the previous exercise, this exercise is designed to shift your point of view in order to develop new ways of thinking about any problems or challenges you are facing. Both exercises can be useful to practice when you are stuck and seeking inner guidance.

Transform into your greater potential

If you are doing your best to make your dream a reality, the journey is going to change you. The 'you' at that destination will not be the same you of today.

You can make this process easier by *consciously* transforming yourself as you progress, so that you deliberately make yourself into the person who is qualified to dwell at the heart of your ultimate goal.

Here's an example. Suppose you're training to play professional basketball, but you're not at that level yet. Suddenly you are placed in a top-level team. Chances are you won't last long, and by the end of the first game you will probably be out of the team because you didn't yet qualify at that level. You're just not there *yet*.

Here's the reality: you can't just magically appear at the end without having first done the work on yourself, to transform yourself into the person who qualifies to reside in that end goal. Yes, you have the potential within you, but you still need to move through a transformational journey to realise that potential.

Therefore you should be doing everything you can to make yourself into that transformed person. Become who you need to be to succeed at your ultimate goal.

This includes taking care of your health through proper diet, sleep, and exercise. It can include resolving any problems in your relationships, your work, your finances, or other aspects of your life. It can mean building your knowledge, skillset, and professional or personal qualities. Do everything you can to make your being and life balanced and capable. Manifesting your destiny and becoming your best self go hand in hand.

Building imagination into the concrete

How you, and those around you, transform as a result of achieving your dreams in the world is most important.

Many people don't know their dreams—they follow the dreams of others. Some may have a sense of their own dreams but lack the desire to achieve them. Very few see their dreams clearly, want them strongly, and work practically toward them.

Just as knowing how to paint is the original ability behind all paintings, as it enables one to produce a real painting from one's vision or imagination, and just as scientific theory is the precondition to scientific experiment, which leads to tangible material outcomes such as new technologies, so knowing how to turn dreams into reality is the original creative purpose behind dreams and an essential skill for realising those dreams.

The world is an endless dynamic exchange of imagination and actuality. As you work toward realising your dream, don't become locked into an abstract idea of what your dream is or should be. Allow your dream to evolve as though it is alive.

An evolving dream is not about adopting a different end goal or completely stopping. It is like seeing the mountain peak more clearly as you approach it, because it is becoming a reality. Among the mists of the valley from where your dream was initially conceived, the details of it were likely vague, more of an idea, an instinct, a feeling. But as you rise higher and gain more capability and capacity to reach your dream, its details become clearer. New facets appear that you were not aware of; new possibilities and paths through which to grow your dream. Your dream is becoming real through your action. It is gaining a foothold in reality.

At this point you need to keep building your dream into the concrete world. But you shouldn't discard the imaginal side of it. Neither should the imaginal and the concrete be chained together, so that one is forced to replicate the other. Both need to breathe, one in the world and one in your soul's imagination.

As the concrete reality of your dream develops, so will your dream evolve. Your dream is a living experience within you that, like creativity, should be given the freedom to naturally develop in response to what you are building in the world. In that way, it becomes real and not just an abstract idea.

Think of a person you admire who had an aspiration to achieve their dream in the world and eventually succeeded in doing this. There are many examples of famous and lesser-known individuals. By achieving their dreams, that person is aligned with their deepest talent, purpose, and meaning in life. Furthermore, they show the world that what is conceivable in the imagination, in one's dreams, is also possible in reality.

Such people—humans just like you and me—demonstrate the implications of achieving one's full potential, including having to face all the challenges that come with that journey.

This in turn can often greatly benefit the wider world. There is nothing innately selfish about pursuing one's own dreams and greater potential. History is full of examples where individuals have successfully followed their calling, leading to some of the greatest discoveries and contributions humankind has ever known.

Turning dreams into reality has a transformative and inspiring effect upon the world. It blends reality and imagination to produce new understandings of what is humanly possible.

It's time to reshape the nest, or leave

Now, we're almost ready to wrap up this section. But before we do that, let's examine your environment.

Sometimes it's not you that is holding you back, but your environment. To advance, you either need to change it or leave it.

There are always bigger worlds, better worlds, greater adventures for yourself and those around you. Yet the human tendency to settle into comfortable spaces, even if they're not particularly comfortable, is ever present.

If you're the type to retire yourself into shallow comforts that don't serve your greater dream, don't let it happen. Make the changes to your environment and lifestyle (your nest) to ensure you have the best circumstances through which to achieve your dream. When you experience that the pursuit of your great dream brings a much deeper, more satisfying internal comfort, superficial distractions that are not aids toward your goal will lose their appeal.

19 Does the nest (the environment and lifestyle) you inhabit have everything you need to best achieve your unique dream? Rate its suitability (1 is least; 10 is most):

    1   2   3   4   5   6   7   8   9   10

What changes can you make to your environment (that are within your ability) so that you can dramatically increase the likelihood of achieving your goal?

_____

_____

_____

If your immediate environment has everything you need, your in a good place. But don't be too quick to assume no changes are needed. The human mind can endlessly justify its own discrepancies. If you have a goal to achieve, then you need to act to ensure that it will come about. This means transforming any factors along the way that hinder that goal.

What about your lifestyle—what changes can you make to increase the likelihood of achieving your goal? **20**

_____

_____

_____

If your environment is preventing you from achieving your goals and cannot be changed, then the better option may be to move to a different environment. If this is needed, what might this move look like?

_____

_____

_____

The other side to this is that sometimes change is used as an excuse to avoid something difficult that must be done: "If only I lived in that house, I would work much harder to reach my goal" … "If I didn't have to clean the house, I could spend more time on my success." Be realistic and smart about such things. Perhaps you could hire a cleaner to free up time and actually work more on your goal. Perhaps by hiring a cleaner, you're just shirking responsibility and in reality you would only end up wasting more time scrolling randomly on your phone.

Give yourself kind, genuine direction, like a wise leader.

Self-imposed limits

This section has focused on preparing for action. You may not have started on your plan yet, and that's perfectly okay. The real action will begin soon. The aim so far has been to outline some of the parameters around action, and to look into what it takes to act effectively. I have provided some tools and understanding to this end, which you can draw from as you work towards your dream.

Your actions, or lack of them, are entirely your responsibility. Too often people become frozen in assumptions around what they can achieve through their own efforts. We base our future on our past, and that includes future limitations based on outcomes from the past. Limiting ourselves, we then look to others to free us.

As a kid, perhaps you took a risky jump on the playground and failed. You forever assume that if you try that jump again, it's going to hurt. So you place a limit on doing that, maybe for good reason to avoid injury. But maybe if you tried again, you would have made it. Life is full of such things. You then grow up to admire (or envy) those who make bold jumps in life. It's easier to spectate.

As we grow older, we may place more and more limits upon ourselves, until we become shut off from our own potential. Not everyone does this—the more adventurous types know that growth requires challenges, pushing the limits, in order to improve. What was not possible yesterday becomes possible today. That is how life grows, and it's scary to some. This is how athletes set new records; how a business owner makes their first million; how a man risks heartbreak to ask a beautiful woman on a date, and they eventually end up happily married.

audentis Fortuna iuvat **("fortune favours the bold") – Virgil**

You may have heard of the baby elephant who is tied to a post with a thin rope, and despite trying with all its strength to break free, is unable to break the rope. The elephant eventually grows into a full sized, five-tonne creature, mighty and powerful. But its mentality is fixed: the rope cannot be broken. As it believes, so it behaves. Its freedom becomes limited by its own mind.

Now this story ignores the ability we all have to learn and grow. It assumes that we remain stuck in the limitations of our past without realising. That is true for many people with unexamined lives. In some circumstances, it's wise to adhere to the lessons of the past—common sense does indeed prevail. But if you are on the path of self-improvement, there are certain instances where you cannot settle for who you were yesterday. If something holds you back simply because you fail to question your assumptions, then maybe it's time to get your curious hat on. If you're working to improve at something, you must keep a fresh, beginner's mind. Don't be the elephant that doesn't realise its greater potential.

Before having achieved something difficult, you may doubt yourself. But if you know where you are going and it's the best destination you have, you must persevere. One you reach it, the doubt will vanish—it was illusory after all. But if you give up prematurely, the doubt becomes real; it sets in your mind like concrete. Then it's much harder to overcome. Not impossible, just harder.

Think back to when you first wrote down your big dream at the start of this book. Did you doubt it? Do you still? If you've completed all the activities well, then you would have done a lot of work on that dream since then. It's likely to have developed into a clearer, more pragmatic map of what you are aiming for, why, and how to get there. If this is truly worth achieving, then take yourself seriously.

You can do it!

The time to climb is now

You've written your vision, formed your goals, and prepared for action. Are you ready then to start on step 1 of your plan? If you are, go for it!

BUT I'M NOT READY ...

If you're not ready, then you need to go back over the earlier sections. Check what you written for your vision and your plan. Ask yourself why you're not ready?

If it's a matter of the details, if there's something that needs correcting in your vision, or something that needs adjusting in your plan, go ahead and adjust it.

If it's a matter of your external environment, resources, timing, or any other factor outside of your control, then these factors should be built into your plan. Go ahead and do this—then return here.

The reality is, there may never be a perfect environment or ideal timing, and you may not have every resource you need to begin the journey. So be flexible and resourceful; find ways to adapt and acquire what you need. Include these as solutions in your plan.

If what's preventing you from starting right now is your own psychological resistance, then you have a choice. Either you find a balanced approach and wisely apply everything you have to work through any resistance. Or, your greatest dream is not for you. Give it up and do what others are doing with their lives, and do your best to enjoy that.

There is no judgement in the latter—you're free to choose whatever you want for yourself. Not everyone is ready to bring about their greatest dreams. Perhaps the time will come later in life.

That said, deciding that your dream is not for you is not at all what this book is about; too many people postpone what is most meaningful to them, for a variety of reasons, and end up with regrets. But the soul does not forget its calling, and life has ways of making this heard.

Sometimes you simply have to start with what you have and trust in yourself. If you are prepared to take on the greatest adventure of your life and strive toward your greatest dream, then you must create solutions to problems as they arise, including internal resistance. Develop creative ways that work for you. Add them into your plan. The first time you apply such a solution may be the most difficult. But the more you exercise your skill in overcoming obstacles, the easier it becomes.

Maybe the solution is coaching, journalling, physical exercise, a psychologist, a pilgrimage? If you really want to achieve your dream, you will do whatever it takes to find the solution needed to overcome any resistance and get yourself on track.

Remember, luck is largely preparation (skill, knowledge, resources, people, plans, and so on), so that when the right circumstances do arise, you can seize the opportunity swiftly and fully.

Your dream isn't going anywhere. If you still experience obstacles to initiating action, take the time to better prepare the way for your dream to become your inevitable reality. Revise your plan accordingly.

Are you ready to climb?

Check that everything is in place and looks good, make use of the tools provided in this book throughout the journey, and start acting on your plan from this moment on.

The time to climb is now!

It is up to you.

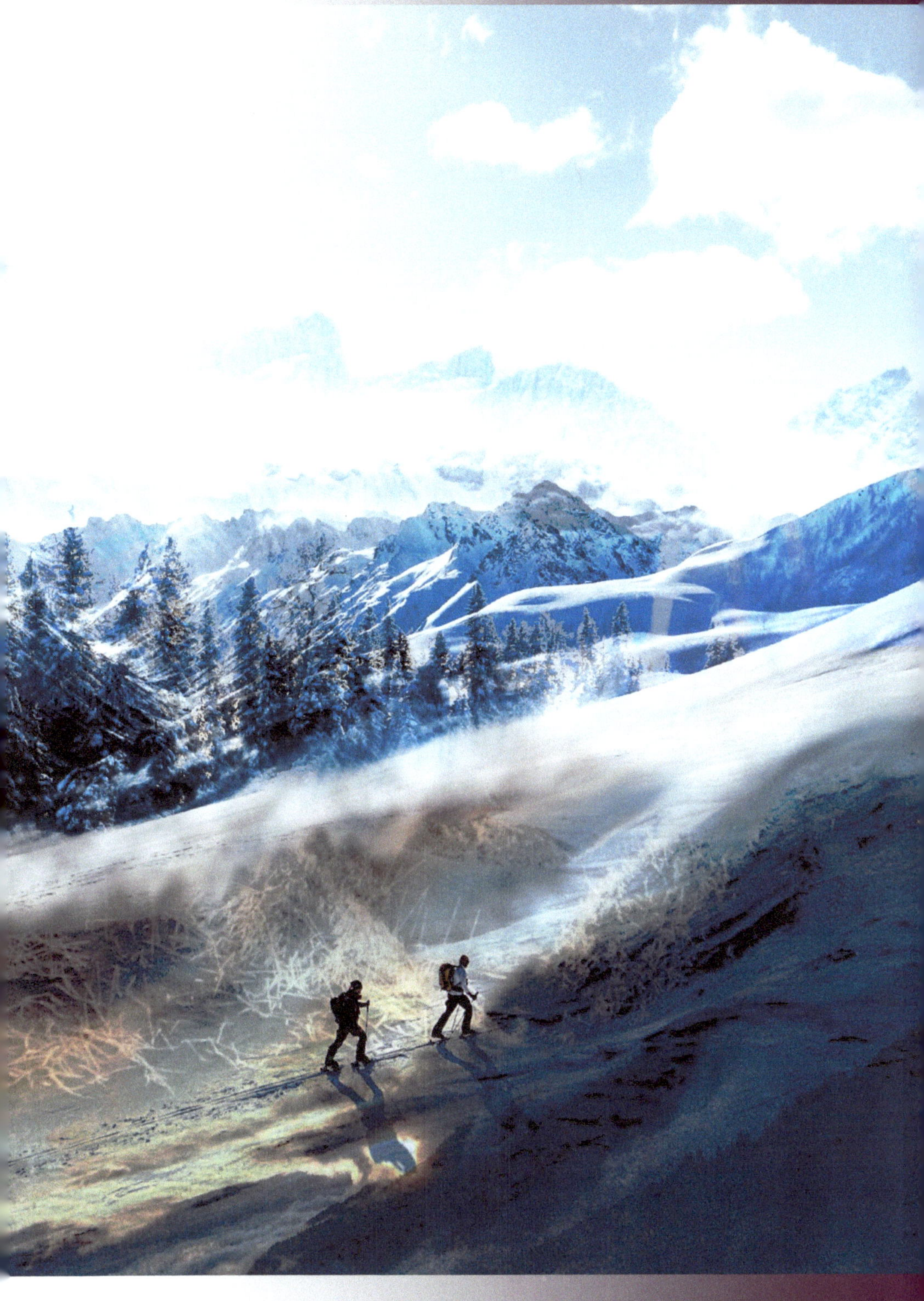

Extras

Epilogue: The peak is forever

When you arrive at your end goal, the peak, you will see there are mountains beyond it. Mountains upon mountains, endless possibilities.

Those mountains may be evolutions of your original dream, or they may be new dreams.

You will (and always do) have the choice as to where you go next, having reached your goal. My recommendation is that you keep going. Evolve your dream further. There's no reason why your end goal should be fixed once you have reached it. Consider how it may develop in new ways. Consider how it can grow to benefit others.

Having achieved your goal, take time to reflect upon the journey you have taken, how it has changed you, enriched your experience, and deepened human connections. Reflect upon the lives you have improved through your work.

By bringing your innermost purpose into the world, you will achieve greatness in human existence. You will have completed a huge part of the puzzle of being human.

Always remember, on each step of the journey, through hardship and ease, and especially when you reach a peak, the experience is sacred.

By sacred, I mean the experience speaks deeply to you in a way that is bigger than anything you've ever known.

To make something sacred is to sacrifice (from the Latin *sacer*, 'sacred, holy', and *faciō*, 'do, make'). To achieve a great dream requires sacrifices—of time, resources, and effort; of personal vices that hold you back; of lesser paths you could have taken.

You may settle on that peak, in the well-deserved ripeness of your sacrifice. But the world will continue turning in its seasons and that peak you've worked so hard to reach will erode over time, like all things, under weathers beyond your control.

As you continue in your life, you will carry those deepest moments of meaning, insight, power, purpose, and contentment that you gathered at the peak, and at the most trying of times, and when you lost and suffered, learnt from it, picked yourself up again, and kept on going until you achieved what was deeply yours and yours only to fulfil in this world.

The rewards of this journey are not superficial. What is most significant to you will make itself known through the power of its resonance with your soul. This is why it's essential to follow your inner compass; to pursue that which excites you the most, stimulates your curiosity, enlivens your imagination, and emboldens your will.

You will experience depth of meaning and purpose as you make your way toward your peak. All the power of that journey will remain alive within you. The innermost gains of your sacrifice become perennial, in your memory, your dreams, and your being. You become a valuable example for others, with the power to contribute to the world around you.

And in time, new, related dreams—those mountains beyond—may call to you from within.

Reader reflections

A place to write your own thoughts as you read.

NOTES, THOUGHTS, REFLECTIONS.

NOTES, THOUGHTS, REFLECTIONS.

NOTES, THOUGHTS, REFLECTIONS.

NOTES, THOUGHTS, REFLECTIONS.

NOTES, THOUGHTS, REFLECTIONS.

NOTES, THOUGHTS, REFLECTIONS.

NOTES, THOUGHTS, REFLECTIONS.

NOTES, THOUGHTS, REFLECTIONS.

References

1. B. Wiese, 'Successful pursuit of personal goals and subjective well-being', in B. Little, K. Salmela-Aro, and S. Phillips (eds.), *Personal project pursuit: Goals, action, and human flourishing*, Lawrence Erlbaum Associates, 2007, pp. 301–328.

2. L. King, J. Hicks, J. Krull, and A. Del Gaiso, 'Positive affect and the experience of meaning in life', *Journal of Personality and Social Psychology*, vol. 90, no. 1, 2006, pp. 179-196.

3. V. Frankl, *The will to meaning: Foundations and applications of logotherapy*, New American Library, 1969.

4. J. Ruffin, 'The anxiety of meaninglessness', *Journal of Counseling and Development*, vol. 63, no. 1, 1984, pp. 40-42.

5. Nasdaq, 'Generational Wealth: Why do 70% of Families Lose Their Wealth in the 2nd Generation?', *Nasdaq, Inc.*, New York, United States, 2018, https://www.nasdaq.com/articles/generational-wealth%3A-why-do-70-of-families-lose-their-wealth-in-the-2nd-generation-2018-10 (accessed 18 December 2023).

Author bio | Dr Todd William Dearing

Founder and Director, Genius Authoring Pty Ltd.

A natural polymath dedicated to self-actualisation, mastery of the art of writing, and life-long learning, Dr Dearing is an experienced writer, researcher, analyst, editor, business professional, and teacher.

He has worked in the private sector, academia, government, and as an entrepreneur and holds a PhD in English and First Class Honours in Art History.

Dr Dearing has over 25 years' experience in pursuit of self-actualisation across a wide range of transformative disciplines and practices, including teaching, researching, and writing in these areas.

As Founder and Director of Genius Authoring, he helps individuals and organisations to reach their greater potential through the art of writing and by communicating knowledge for personal, professional, and cultural transformation.

Genius Authoring is a research organisation dedicated to human potential through the art of writing.

We provide publications and professional document services so that individuals and organisations can reach their greater potential.

Our vision is to establish a wiser, more articulate, and more adventurous humanity.

For more information, visit: **www.geniusauthoring.com.au**

Nothing is.
Everything is becoming.

– Heraclitus

www.ingramcontent.com/pod-product-compliance
Lightning Source LLC
Chambersburg PA
CBHW042226090526
44585CB00001BA/5